FRANCIS TIAIN-STEEL

GLIDE ABOVE THE SEA

(C) & (P) Versatility Publishing 2009

Glide Above The Sea by Francis Tiain-Steel

First Edition

ISBN - 978 - 557 - 08486 - 9

Some Friends

Dean Sobers
Zane Kanderian
Drew Benvie
Will Corner
Dave Mitchell
For All At Sonfire
Joyce & Jo

Some Family

Mum & Dad Steel
Jen Steel
Clifford Moorhouse
David & Beryl Symons
Christine Beardsell
All of the Steel relatives

Foreword

The seminal poems that were created between 2000 and 2008 in Tiain-Steel's first collection of poems were the start of his personal and intimate account of love and loss related by way of hindsight, melancholy, yet somehow full of hope. They were stylised in the form of a nouvelle beat poetry, and Kadija Sesay coined the term 'Jazz Poetry' or 'Prose poetry', because they told stories and charted and watermarked emotions in their entire spectrum whilst creating poetry free of structure but full of imagery and wordplay.

The new collection created between 2007 and 2009 are known as the Metaphysical Poems with the title 'Glide Above The Sea' named as a reference to Neil Young lyrics.

The use of verse continues in its spontaneity, and borrows more techniques from the 60's beat authors and crosses it over into poetics. Umi Sisquane named 2009 'the year of the prophets of verse...' But Tiain-Steel is using his themes and content the central and pivotal meter of is book.

In *Glide Above The Sea*, he creates a home for the soul which does not rely on religion per say; but very much to ethereal moments that we all have at memorable or poignant moments in life, that we often find ourselves unconsciously aiming for yet often only get a rare glimpse of. It owes itself to the mystical tradition of spirituality whereby these moments are not evoked but come spontaneously when we least expect it and when we least pursue them. Living spirituality and religion; free, unconditional, and available to anyone...and full of mystery.

In addition to that it creates a place where we can feel comfortable with recalling these moments and glide with them, rather than feel a sad nostalgia, but a freedom to remember, enjoy, and continue knowing this halcyon-ia is part of us.

I hope you enjoy the new collection, and look forward to writing the next collection.

INDEX

1. From Sunlit To Dust
2. There Are Shadows Outside My Door
3. Nujibes In The Winter Air
4. The Skin Turned Blue
5. Xylophonic

6. A Small Lite In A Dark Sky
7. Seeing Stars…Not Seeing Scars
8. The Fields Are Burning
9. And There Surrounds A Fence
10. Trust For Laughs
11. Love Is
12. Philosophy Of Music
13. Seven Clouds
14. Three Colours: Red
15. Sunbruised
16. The Physicist's Success
17. The Philosopher's Success
18. Beer = ….
19. Dead Man
20. The Physicist's Love
21. The Artist's Love
22. Sitting in a darkened room
23. Three Colours : White
24. One Horse Town
25. Queens Of Black Hearts
26. Games
27. September
28. All I Knew
29. Light And Dark
30. Three Colours : Blue
31. The Healer
32. The Diamond Eyes

33. Stonecasters And Spells

34. Goodbye

From Sunlit To Dust

Like a satellite falling…to earth,

Earthbound lights caress the sky,

But only at night can you see them

Then your eyes are open to the

Reflective stars surrounding me,

If only….

…my light was bright, but my age,

Covers the lamp like a small dark cloud,

And aloud thunder cracks and lightning

Breaks back across the scattered dust,

Like memories in a timer,…sand gone,

I wander as I wonder yonder lost,

As the haze dispersed – curse removed,

I see you….I see you again,

And then gone,

A split glass across the skyline,

And then foregone…bygones be gone,

And passes by.

You sheltered me on a lonely night,

When all was thread bare, and there

We kissed, in a moonlight's tide.

I wonder where you are now,

Fallen satellite in an October sky.

There Are Shadows Outside My Door

Darklight, no life, wooden boards,

And split windows, splinters enters

Sinews,

There are shadows outside my door;

Rain clouds, whispering loud,

In runes gowns, pointing round,

Passing down,

There are shadows outside my door;

Enemies at the gates,

Filled with hate, lies and taddled fate,

Bullying when suffering,

Severing words in the distant glaze,

There are shadows outside my door.

Black and white, no middle,

Soul left, cruelly meant,

Severance like an effervescent spell

Tearing things down,

There are shadows outside my door.

You have no need,

But still you read and point one

Finger one way and three the other,

There are now shadows outside your door.

Nujibes In The Winter Air

I hear voices aloud and clear, that are

Near in sound and distant in tone,

The fear the twist my soul has gone,

And the river has run dry,

I die a thousand times, to return to

College times, but I see, those

That are long gone, pictured in my mind;

At night the tears of a winter sky,

Cold – rest on my cheeks – but coals

Orange and down-glowing, are not

Warm enough.

The floor in here is rough and the

Diamonds in her eyes are smooth,

Like how she talks…when I'm around,

But go black when I turn around;

For reasons unknown to me,

I leave, like the autumn trees,

To naked and bare, and

The cold gaze of the son, doesn't

Even win some dignity for me.

I die a thousand times, and still

Our paths don't cross,

I am lost like the noon day sun.

The Skin Turned Blue

The earth is green and the sky is grey,

Today…dear friend, your skin is blue;

Once your heart beat ran fast,

And we gathered behind the bar,

Laughing….asking questions…no answers;

Two years after….you died,

My mind was spiraled, and my

Eyes were red with death,

My hair a mess,

You were better friend - then known,

When I was well, and you were dew,

Fresh and alive like the grass,

I'm sorry you left early.

The day your skin tone….got lighter,

Eyes when whiter, mine went redder,

Those changes were for ever;

And ever amen

Then I wrote….two years after…

Dead to the world,

I knew you were some way ahead,

My eyes now pink and less well read.

Xylophonic

I remember in a mid-March, 2001;
When I came back from Cardiff,
I was smiling and laughing,
Surrounded by my friends,
And thought the limits had no end
To the sky,
I thought I could reach up and fly,
My mind was fixed, and my heart
was strong,
We walked along to Howard's way
And it was a party,
Chatting till dawn,
It was the ground beneath the floor,
It was all we needed,
I listened to two songs with
Ambience, two long instrumentals,

And they remind me of you,
And remind you of me,
You were more than some girl met at the party.

A Small Lite In A Dark Sky
We met on a dark night of the soul,
Your eyes were dark, with lights shining in
Them,
I jumped in them and they closed
Delicately,
We were in company for the sake of company's
Sake,
It wasn't a one night date,
Maybe then I left it too late,
But hey; life goes on, especially in those eyes.
Like a small pair of stars in a dark sky.

Seeing Stars…Not Seeing Scars

The deep dark blue of just after dusk,
I see fortune and glory beheld
In my stars, no longer turning
To the past to count my scars,
Live and let livings my dream,
See stars and not scars,
But I see the blanketing,
And the sun's last blaze,
Before it ducks down to see another day,
Another start, another life on the
Other side of the world,
I turn on my heels,
And walk across the fields then
Back on to the streets,
See stars not scars, that'll make my week,
Month, year, decade, half century, life, and on….
But the sky is clear.

The Fields Are Burning

Rivers have run dry,
The waters have rolled back...
The rock yields no stream,
And there is no chance of rain,
And my staff is bent,
Chiselled away,
My sandals are split,
And the flask is full -
Of sand from this rough terrain.

I look across the plains,
And the fields are dry,
The river runs with blood,
There is a mountain of sand,
And when I open up my heart,
It is full of scars.

And There Surrounds A Fence

For fifteen days and nights, I sit

And mediate, on nothing,

Only my mind is so trusting but finds

The likelihood of hope disguising it's

Self of Light; covered by darkness,

A winter kiss and green earths's bliss

Gone in the mist.

My sorrow is engaged to the desert,

And wilderness crumbles.

I stumble upon vast shores, that

are adorned with more love than can be

Imagined,

But I'm uninvited, and there are

Voices in this land.

And they're surrounded by a fence,

They're meant to be well-meant

But they're hell-bent, fury

Without (Selah).

Think before you speak,

They reek before they do, with

Havoc, and have it large,

I have no part…here.

Trust For Laughs

Over the hills of the north,

And into the horizon we journeyed,

Only earning a pittance, worthy

Of a laugh,

But our task is not fair, it's a mask

A mask, with broad-bent grin,

Like a dark knight story, making me

Uneasy, and the chaos

Ensues when they open their mouths

And move from the script.

One dance floor party watched from

Around the edges and fringes,

By men in black long coats,

Spotting for trouble, not knowing

They are the worst kind of jin.

They talk of things small and use the

Word 'devil' and 'sin', not noticing

That speaking of that, brings it in.

I was suffering, and they were

Muttering rhymes of all kinds,

Of vent, as if they were the centre

Of the Ark's tent.

Well-met, but not well-meant,

Thinking they were heaven-sent,

But gave off a firey-scent,

Of sulphur, and acidic ulcers.

Fair well, supreme f(r)iends.

Love Is

Love is high, love is low,

Love is sky, love is slow,

Love is time, love is riverflow,

Love is fine, love is home.

Love is vast, love is wide,

Love is fast, love is tide,

Love is laughs, love is trying,

Love is cast, love is flying.

Love is in, love is out,

Love is skin, love is doubt,

Love is bring, love is how,

Love is wings, love is clouds.

Love is above, Love is below,

Love is the ground, love is show,

Love is mountains, love is fountains,

Love is the direction through the doubting,

Love is care, love is kiss,

Love is in the sea for what we fish,

Four ways, north south, east west;

In all these regions love is the best.

The thing we hope for, the thing through which

We rest.

Philosophy Of Music

The sound of waves floating round,

Like a sea that has found its land

To come in on, landing,

Music makes my heart pound,

And gives it understanding,

When at a gig, there air is full,

Yet it clearing,

Makes memories connect, and

No future fearing,

Music pressed against our chests.

I do my best….my love is for you,

So come through again,

And I'll play it on the guitar again,

I lift my hand and place it in yours,

Eventhough past has passed I still

Adore.

I kind of miss you,

But move on to find more,

Music playing in my ears.

Yesteryear, tomorrow's year,

I'll find one's more.

Seven Clouds

Lying on one's back staring at the sky,

Clouds passing by and I count

The times that the sun shines…through,

The grey and the black,

I'm not afraid of that,

But now, rain came and went,

I just lay there till it passed by,

I smile,

(She must be a thousand miles from here)

No trial too great,

But thanks to the seven of my closest,

I got through, I remember you,

And I thank you, my friends and fam,

Seven Clouds sheltering the sky,

From hostile lands.

Xylophonic

I remember in a mid-March, 2001;

When I came back from Cardiff,

I was smiling and laughing,

Surrounded by my friends,

And thought the limits had no end

To the sky,

I thought I could reach up and fly,

My mind was fixed, and my heart

was strong,

We walked along to Howard's way

And it was a party,

Chatting till dawn,

It was the ground beneath the floor,

It was all we needed,

I listened to two songs with

Ambience, two long instrumentals,

And they remind me of you,

And remind you of me,

You were more than some girl met at the party.

A Small Lite In A Dark Sky

We met on a dark night of the soul,

Your eyes were dark, with lights shining in

Them,

I jumped in them and they closed

Delicately,

We were in company for the sake of company's

Sake,

It wasn't a one night date,

Maybe then I left it too late,

But hey; life goes on, especially in those eyes.

Like a small pair of stars in a dark sky.

I tried to remember why the flat seem so

Bare, full of warm inside,

But the ceiling permeated lies.

You left only three days before,

Ignoring the sneering and laughing,

That seeped into the sands of time

Outside,

I definitely could see the sun in the sky,

But it was a drought, the only liquid

Spilt were from the roaming ronins

Outside, pouring and outpouring

With leary leers, to hide their tears from

Every fear they saw in their own eyes,

every time they glimpsed in the mirror.

This place was no riveria,

But in some ways it was,

I kissed you goodbye, and we cried.

Then you left. I long to see you soon.

High above, the clouds conspired,

And rain loomed,

Wind swayed the trees,

And your taxi was away.

Seeing Stars...Not Seeing Scars

The deep dark blue of just after dusk,

I see fortune and glory beheld

In my stars, no longer turning

To the past to count my scars,

Live and let livings my dream,

See stars and not scars,

But I see the blanketing,

And the sun's last blaze,

Before it ducks down to see another day,

Another start, another life on the

Other side of the world,

I turn on my heels,

And walk across the fields then

Back on to the streets,

See stars not scars, that'll make my week,

Month, year, decade, half century, life, and on….

But the sky is clear.

Three Colours: Red

A man, called Red.

Red like his eyes,

He tried to walk in a straight line.

Red, he had rum tonight, his was meeting his love.

Tonight would be the night, he felt as he marched down Fair Street,

The heat of the summer's set before him, he was lost in dusk;

Enough of the beauties and babes, enough of the one night stands,

He mused and made plans that this would be the one – the only one.

Mystified by how he found her, blinded by a morning star;

He had seen those green eyes amongst many black bleary I'd pairs

In many a grotty bar on southside. He saw her there with

Friends and foes, eyeing those who eyed her with a slight discomfort at
The drunkenness and wrecklessness of uninhibited man's wild
Attempts to close on first, second, third, fourth base efforts.
Varying success he had had with many before her. But this night he had no dutch courage
Because he was skint, he had had a skin full the night before,
And made valiant efforts to repair the damage to his former
Misspent love. She wouldn't call back,
But he rang for the last time before she answered – he got his answer,
Which cut to the bone. Like a horse in a race,
Over many steeples, but fallen by the wayside,
Now ready to be put out of his misery. His misery
Left him once he saw the only one, his true one,
Some stars pierced the night as he walked through Beach Road, recollecting
The first night he had seen her.
She flirted a smile, and a caring glance before the throngs
Moved by and the night swirled,

Curly had had to much to drink, shots a plenty, he was

Sick over a girls new shoes, but true to form,

He apologized, and somehow managed to take her home.

Red continued down Priory Lane, she had offered to meet him

Again. he was gliding, like the tide in his mind.

Small lights in a dark sky line,

Broke through a cyan night.

His gracelessness was met with a joyous haze,

At the delight of seeing her again. He harped back to the time of

His gaining of this love.

Curly had gone home early,

A burly bouncer had ushered him out,

Like the star dj that he was. Lost

In a motorcade of fans fair accolades.

He was made up for tonight, but Red was left

Alone by the bar, skint…sober…depressed.

A drunken skunk of chunk, pressed against him

And asked him to dance, to which he politely denied,

And once gone wondered why he always got the

Not the monkeys but the peanuts.

He looked across the floor to the green eyed leaf

Dancing to and fro on the disco stage.

He felt drunk, love punch drunk.

Then a Brad Pitt kissed her and his heart sunk.

He wondered if or when…but then a good friend

Came onto the scene and stood in his line of eye's fire.

'Jay, good to see you…'

And the conversation went on about Herbie Hancock, Miles Davies,

Nina Simone, Bobby Humphrey; which was shouted over the pop clash,

Punk trash, crap coming over distorted speakers.

Jay was cool.

Never out of place with his words,

But sometimes he was out of words in this place.

'Shit music, huh?'

He knew everybody, and Red decided to ask him who the green eyed leaf

Was from across the wayside.

Jay, tried to ascertain with a gaze.

'I don't her name. But she's beautiful, I think I'm gonna bang her...'

True to form.

But he met a stallion's glare.

'Oh, you like her. I'll do some research.'

He treated things like a leaf on a mission, a mission…missing it

For a while he returned with a statement.

'She works at The London Bar.'

Then catching the attention of a red haired dancer breaking into

The crowd, he disappeared onto the dance floor.

Red continued down Priory Lane recollecting seeing the green eyed

leaf,

Move back and forth, with her Brad Pitt type along side.

She had blond hair, terrific smile,

Which lit up the corner of the room,

The foggy haze of smoke (before the ban),

Panned through the club's air, but her smile parted it like

The sea.

Red went to the gents to gather perspective and to move on,

A dark haired beauty was outside, smoking, and

Fuming, at the same time.

She winked casually.

'Do you want a drink?' she asked.

'I'm not drinking to tonight.'

(Well you can buy me one then...). Red read between

The lines.

As they walked out of the cue to get a drink,

He went to the bar, confident....if but for a moment,

Before looking into the corner again.

He turned round and split Fumer's drink all over Green Leaf.

The Brad Pitt Type postured, and stooped aggressively.

'See what you've done,'

'It's okay,' Green Leaf said.

(I'll have buy a new top...). Red read between

The Lines.

He had spilt red red wine all down her pristine white top.

Fumer and Pitt got into a slanging match,

A rally that lasted all of a minute but seemed like a

Life time.

In these moments the world seemed to slow

Down for Red: one because of him, but mainly because of the green

eyed leaf,

Who was now smiling back at him.

Before time returned to regular play speed,

And Pitt dragged her off into the crowd.

'What a dick!' said Red.

(What a bitch! Said Fumer). Red, quite red, read between

The lines.

The sex with Fumer had been great,

But something was missing,

She had a smile that was there,

But was not.

She had eyes that sparkled,

But not with light.

She clasped his chest and lit up

A cigarette,

She was smoking and fuming.

She vented about everything that

Was wrong….

With the world…

With her…

With her family.

The closet was now open and could never be shut.

But Red, thought,

She is alright.

His subconscious thought

Is She alright?

His heart felt

Is she all right?

He knew,

But his libido said

To them all

("Shut the fuck up…

And listen and nod…

And *you'll* be alright")

Red read between the bed line(n)

And played again.

Priory Lane came to an end, and

He came onto Station Road.

He walked with a stagger in his step.

Fumer was now his lady, but leaf only looked on;

And then the wind took her off with Brad;

Fumer was his lay…

Sunbruised

The sun was bruised with a grey and black shiner,

It dipped in behind a blanket,

And then it shivered,

Summer was grey again.

I looked out my window onto,

Grey and purple light, the delight

Of the spring was gone -

Because I was still, still, water

Creeping down the sides of the windows.

Lowly I and my SDD came back with

A vengeance; just and the depth of light

Became a problem. But not only for me,

Some of the

Anthropolati, felt the same way as me,

In a manner less way of speaking.

But for me as well, the light reflected off

My skin in a way they didn't like,

I would have been better in cricket…you

Know when you've been tango'd.

Because they weren't white either,

They were bruised orange and sometimes

Shoe leather brown.

It was the black tango can declaring the guiness

The wrong colour.

I think they take too much sugar….

But I was in a safe house, where their stones

Could reach,

They wondered around beneath like morlocks,

But with less soft hands.

The sun came out again and the locusts

Scattered, and my shattered anatomy

Gathered the…

Strength to carry on for another day.

Hopefully will shine brighter soon,

Assuming it does not flicker tears

On all of us…unassumed.

The Physicist's Success

(Age + Confidence - Rejection + Alcohol) = Sexual Success,

(Friendship+Confidence+Sense Of Humour)-(Fallouts)³+ (Makeups) = Social Success,

(Sex Education + Experience with Good Women) - (Experience whilst thoroughly pissed) - (Sex when without protection)² + (Good girlfriends)³ - (Bad Girlfriends X Bad Laddish Friends) = Sexual Health Ratio,

The Philosopher's Success

I worked on this ratio for thirty two years,

All of my fears and failures came over me,

But I realised that I'm free to find the right lady,

When there isn't so much alcohol within me.

Success is not needing to write the logical formula

In the first place.

But it's late, I've got a guest,

So I better check my breath and which

The rest of you a good night.

(I'm getting layed tonight...aha!)

Beer = ...

Beerfear on = Too much weed with alcohol.

Beergoggles on = Very bad mistakes.

Beergoogles on = Very bad mishapes online.

Beergodles on = Trying it on with the local born agains ladies. More chance of getting converted, than breaching the iron skirt.

Beergogos on = Ending up in strip club, expensive and costly in every sense of the word.

Beerlocos on = Ending flipping out or or going temporarily insane with the one you love or the one you potentially love present.

Beergollum on = A horrible sweaty mess that sends you into a desperate and creepy manner including trying it on (and being turned down by) with every women in the sweaty club.

Beeroes on = Alcohol induced powers evolved from watching too many Heroes episodes, which involves saving a damsel in distress, the result being damsel ok, and you in accident and emergency with a broken pelvis.

Beergoings on = Alcohol induced mess in which a group of you finish drinking and walk home (approx 3 miles), but one takes a random single bus ride to St Ives, Cornwall (approx 200 miles out of the way)

And has no recollection of the journey or indeed how he got back.

But he does have a stolen Ben Nicholson sculpture in his front room.

Beergoingoingonn on = Alcohol induced catatonia where in the space of one minute you've entered a large super club with f®iends, who ditch you or accidently lose you once inside. You stay till the end hoping to find them, not even knowing, that your cool disinterest in the women makes you a little more sexually desirable than usual. But you're too drunk and socially paranoid to notice.

Deadman

One way trip as the train carries forth,
All the folk looker rougher as nearer we draw,
A public hanging commences as we reach our stop;
The town of Machine is where all things cost.
Like a man to his grave he waded out to shore,
Carried on to his otherworld as an outlaw,
Doors open to the river to find his way home,
Yes, he is a long way from there, and

A long way to fall.

The Physicist's Love

(Age + Confidence - Rejection + Alcohol) = Sexual Success,

(Friendship+Confidence+Sense Of Humour)-(Fallouts)^3+ (Makeups) = Social Success,

(Sex Education + Experience with Good Women) - (Experience whilst thoroughly pissed) - (Sex when without protection)^2 + (Good girlfriends)^3 - (Bad Girlfriends X Bad Laddish Friends) = Sexual

Health Ratio,

I worked on this ratio for thirty two years,
All of my fears and failures came over me,
But I realised that I'm free to find the right lady,
When there isn't so much alcohol within me.

Success is not needing to write the formula
In the first place.
But it's late, I've got a guest,
So I better check my breath and which
The rest of you a good night.
(I'm getting layed tonight…aha!)

The Artist's Love

I have a muse but have nothing to lose by

Saying she is as bright as a noon day sky.

As smile at the rain clouds parting and leaving

Only the Son to come out, my eyes turn bright,

It like the northern lights, and up there there were

Plenty.

My muse is a long way from here, but so are the

Stars and I reach from them day in and day out,

Leaving nothing but cloud or mist in my hands.

But the stars sometimes fall and I wish upon them,

So I do with my muse.

I ring her and ask if we can chat -better than that

She says she'll meet me at an old café - heartbeating as

The delicate tone of a soul who is my soul's predicate

On the phone, she smiles and laughs even though she makes it

A date/meeting She's long gone; the fleeting conversation is on, my mind tells me.

'Do you still date artists?' I asked.

'Successful ones.'

'Ah,' I said, 'Could I have the bill please.'

Sitting in a darkened room

Beers craters in my longing for a existential reality,

Outside snow sings along the road with a

Delicate kiss on the surface of concrete subsidiary,

There is a sense of loss,

Where at most my Lord of Hosts comes in a

Pillar of smoke, but

It may or may not have a fire,

The spires have a disclaimer on my soul,

The maker and the runner of life is in all …

But more in the tall towers that need green paper

But I need my soul.

We handshake over the table, which I may

Later regret…(or not…)

Still I'm hearing and I understand the tragic wait,

Nevertheless the small dark room

In a prison – a temple of doom.

I'm sitting in a darkened room,

But I can still see the sky but

There are no stars.

There are no stars.

No laughs in the room

Until I step out.

Darkened room curtains torn wide, and wander through the

Bottles and glass and out the door,

Winter clothes clasped around me,

It is cold a dark room, left to be cleared.

Later on that day….

As I step out streets shimmer,

And more of the sky curesses my gloom,

Lifting it…lifting…till my feet move

Delicately across the snowy lanes,

And my boots warm again.

It is cold on the frosts, but not as frosty as inside,

And a plane wanders by above.

I'm going somewhere new…

Three Colours : White

The sun went down over blue seas,

The estuary was fine from here,

The grains of sand drew back in,

Then forward through into the tide

And far from near.

So I drew down next to the campfire

Burning,

I was learning everything I needed to

Know

About Chloe and all the other girls,

I took a stick prodded the glow,

And ashes flowed and new warm...

Slow Lee grew as Chloe grinded on him,

As the trance beats thumped in, sweat poured

In the summer night heat,

I could feel it from my cotton seat,

Torel lay next to me as the sky

Slowly turned from

Orange to red

To blue to black,

She lay her leg against mine.

The sky seemed black from here,

I had a void in my stomach,

Crampier than the lobster lunch,

(Torel wanted to give me a fish supper),

The cramps punched,

Intestines crunched,

My back hunched,

Then my throat expanded, and a

Foul bitter elixia came up after

Doing its job,

Torel took a sip of her wine,

Jiggled her hips then – she was so fine -

Got up…'I'm bored',

Smiled then went

Off to dance,

I lay there staring at the sky,

Counting over whys and wherefores,

Whilst many poor hornies asked

For me to dance more on the sandy

Floor.

(It was my loss, not theirs)

I went onto to care about everything,

But everything would not care for me,

I wanted to reach God,

But god could not reach me,

I lit up a cigarette before putting out,

And then staring at the clouds looming

Over Ursa Major,

I watched the ironic tie between my

Mind and the sky, breath of winds moving

And then breakingforth into a haze.

(The clouds; grey,

At least it wasn't rain)

My mind on what the gods had told me

Through the teachers, which didn't seem to

Add up, but I would go along,

And join the throngs who came to

Do worship at their congregation.

They had already taken I lot of

Money off me.

(God says give me your money,

And let me give you milk flowing

From the land of sweet honey)

This wasn't going anywhere because,

I had a lot to lose, and

This decision was as blind as

The night sky,

As deep as the sea,

And as tall the cedar trees.

I was in the middle of a party,

I was eighteen, and there

Were drunk girls,

And I was surrounded by best

Friends…how come I'm…

The time past me by.

But eventhough my luck was down,

I could see far past the clouds,

I had it all....I...had it all,

I now I'd lost it again.

But could I ask for anything more?

Joining a cult, could I ask for anymore?

(Cult = My sorrow = guilt = fear)

Jakman came over to me to see

That I had a lot but he saw the tears,

He saw the sunken back,

He took me back in the chairs – away we sat,

After this he slandered me from

Behind,

These narrow trees bend,

Before there is much I have lent –

And I owed, but the weight on

My back is hellbent on crushing me.

Fools rush in the to bulls in the lake

In the field behind our house,

Which centrally placed on the lane,

Where have those wives (desperate),

Slying peering through curtains drawn,

Across from across the road.

4 Miles distant from town,

Not a city but a garbage mound.

Ah, now I've found peace, that

I have been robbed from, I heave-ho.

The lowdown on the down low of my

Mind,

I cry at night, when no one hears,

Were the words that came out of her mouth,

I only said what because of the loud

Music coming out of the stereo about

400 miles north from that town,

In that place, I wore clown make up,

To hide a life performance – hooters

For music and paper for water,

And a car that fell apart at will.

I am still vexed at that text that

My neighbour(?!) sent which read

Pls dnt rng me am nt gng 2 meet.

Well I predictively text an f u with a

Fuck you, who I fucked, who then

Proceeded to fuck me over and

Resultantly fucked me up.

But the sand in the moonlight is white,

Tee came over and kissed me;

If only I had stayed with her…

One night; in a moon's delight.

One Horse Town

I'm slumbering on my floor,

Ignoring the anthropics shouting

Outside my door,

I'm on the planet of the apes,

Except they only share one horse,

And the planet is flat,

And rides the back of a reptile,

And is the size of a town.

I am slow, and I dive down,

Living alone in a one horse town.

Queens Of Black Hearts

She is tall, and there is a stare about her,

Is she angry, or is she just mean,

She wanted to be the queen of all she surveyed;

And she conquered some,

And murdered others…

Some of us rebelled and stood our ground,

But still we live in caves, wondering

When the drought will past,

The name of the queen was on the

Flags, and her king did whatever she

Pleased.

She asked and she received, or so

She believed,

She grabbed and demanded, and

Many a grasp to supplanted

Kingdoms, treasures and jewels.

Her name was ever belled from

The temples of sages of all times,

She dyed lonely and alone,

But fought to live on.

Her fingers were midas like,

But her claws turned gold to…

Dust and mites.

I called her before it came,

The weathered face had

Changed her, so blond hair

To silver,

Green eyes to grey.

She cried…as her song played,

And throngs came to chant her name.

'I've learnt through disgrace…' she said.

'I give up this place, to gain mine in heaven,

If its not too late…'

I paused. 'Never it is,' I said.

Games

Hey, about when your beauty shined

Through…the many faces here,

I, went through the skies and pined,

For…the times our love so clear.

Wait, for me in Clock café,

Make, another card for me,

I'm late, but we all make mistakes,

And the games, you're playing won't change

This.

Lies, have turned our love too blind,

Cries, of when you scuba dived,

Time, of t.v.'s glimpse of you,

True, but only half of you… so move.

Now, the time has passed again,

Then, I will come clean with rain,

All the e-mails are the same,

Same old same old games

You played.

Goodbye, good luck,

Luck....Not riddance.

September

Waiting for my film, to turn on the tv,

Waiting for my love to come and see me,

Storing up the pros, and all of the lines,

Still an agrophobe, but making my best.

Listening in, to all the xenophobes,

And the simian prose, that comes out of mouths,

Finding my own way, in a vasey-town,

Only thing to see is jesus freaks and clowns.

September,

September,

Not the best of...

Times to remember.

All I Knew

And all I knew, has been since two,

And when they fought me,

As they were supposed to,

Old psalms, stayed till the end,

Bad friends, remind me to stay (zen)

The waiting, turned me inside out,

And I asked my gods…

…if they cared for all?

And I drove 100 miles, to see my old

Love at Stockton,

And we wrote 100 times, to see that it

Had no station.

Old throngs, warred till the end,

Bad men, remind me to stay (zen),

And the waiting made me make a call,

To my newly loved…

…was there some care for all?

Light And Dark

Can you feel the ursa minor...

Shining higher than the stars?

Can you feel the shining jewel...

Moving farther far away?

My god of the flux of the stars…

…still I flutter on my back.

Three Colours : Blue

And then the music played on like a jester's

Flute, the king of fools,

Benny was playing pool in a fool's paradise,

He and Jason weren't potting any,

Even though there were many women around

That night,

Ben had had a lot to drink, and was thinking about

The girl he had seen at his last house party.

He had made her as tape, and her name was Adora,

And he adored her,

Only he rung in the week and she hadn't

Answered…she seemed to have ignored him…her

Attitude had pulled at Ben strings…of the heart.

He laughed at Jason's jokes, in an effort to sound

Cheery, but leery guys were catching all the rye…

On their hooks;

And the girls were biting.

Ben saw Adora sitting in the corner with a well

Dressed man,

Sadly Ben went over to talk to her, she said nothing,

He found it tragic, and he went back to the table,

Legs unstable, eyes on his naval he tucked in his

Stomach.

This was a bad night.

Time passed, and Jason scored a bullseye with a tall
Blond woman behind the bar.
Apparently he had said nothing to her, just handed her
His phone and smiled.

Eventually, Adora came over to chat to Ben, whom she
Apologised to.
He loomed over the pool table, eyes jettison, sparkle
Put out.

Adora looked into Ben's eyes, 'Do you still like me?'
Ben looked away, only to see her for dust, as she
Walked over to the bar, after she noticed another
Man…
She was not to be adored.
He put down the pool cue, and walked out of the bar,
He had sobered up in more ways than one;
And she was it….

The Healer

He believed in the one; and the one had

Touched his hand,

His plan was to heal-raise,

(So get out your cheque books!)

He had the power to restore,

And bring life to the dead,

If he had knocked on heaven's door,

He would have brought many back.

So get out your cash!

But when he lost his faith,

He felt at death's door,

His sorrow the cause,

Only when he let go,

Could he move on, and be

Commited to a life of giving…

…for free.

Pythagorean Love

The Hypotenuse is the longest angle of a triangle,

But there's no maths in a love triangle;

Just pointy and sharp ends…

We dance together, you and me;

Until I find out that you're in love with the

Other guy on the other stage;

You're dancing near but look the other way.

We sleep together, you and me;

And we 'span' time, until you're phoning the

Other guy on the other line,

You answer my calls when you're feeling shy.

You ask me what I should do with you,

I write songs, but you give me blues;

Your boyfriend is now the one for you,

But you come to me when he burns his fuse.

Bermuda Triangle,

Yet fully seen,

By all but me,

Bermuda Triangle

Even you see it

Clearly more than me.

The Diamond Eyes

The starlight in your eyes burn bright,

And on this night, and share our love

Under the canoped sky, laden with clouds,

Above there are night birds flying amongst

Garden trees, chasing berries.

We are merry almost drunk on love,

Till we see that there is still more to come.

The star spell a plough above a cloud out

To work.

There are signs in the air, just like everywhere,

My mind isn't heavy,

she's my lover, or at

Least I like to think so.

We sit still on the hill and watch ships

Cast out to sea,

We smile and kiss with lips glistening,

Till dusk turns to dawn.

All for One and one for one. I give my all.

<u>The Shadowland Poet</u>

The music ran as your rhetoric landed

On your lips,

You had soul, not northern, not southern,

But inner, you smiled

Even when you knew of death,

Old and fired, but not tired, but

Everything tried, you're full of life.

May your poem live on even when you go.

Slowly, the poem plays on,

Like a song of a motorcade somewhere,

When I wasn't there, but shelves

Left bare, in a handspun gown,

Even when skint you went to town, on

The other poets on show,

But you can recite, play, and direct…

You still are the best.

Shadows move over you

But you don't fear; they define you.

True poet of the

Shadowlands.

Stonecasters And Spells

The sound of cloud drowsy in it's

Scattering of shardes like glass,

The group stand quietly in a circle,

And only the thunderclaps that strike

Above savages their savaged hair,

That have blood on their foreheads.

I look one glance more at the lady

Called the whore,

But this village misrest near the cliffs of

A distant isle, shows how

The scattering of rocks on the grass,

Eyed careful are beauty;

Like this poor lady in the centre of the centrifugal

Of rocks.

Eventually she drops dead in the bloody grass,

And the parson leads the crowd back out on the town.

I am a scribe,

It is the year 1509,

And I feel as though it's 1059,

And that the village is full of blood.

Goodbye

I walk along the streets with my head down low,

My progression is slow, and I sigh like the air

In sky when high pressure meets low.

I'm alone tonight as my friends are miles (away),

And my fake ones start to hide.

Religion is the end of me, but spirituality is the

Beginning, acting like a man with two cheeks to

Many offered.

Struck on both sides, and my enemy on the sly,

But I down care anymore,

I'll just their ground will break into the core,

But I have no hate to badones, even though they

Cheat and lie and cheat, all I have to do is turn the

Other cheek.

Find a community without disunity,

Find a place that speaks to you, instead ones that speak about

You.

I fly across the halls and into new beginning, with the path

Of least resistance.

To the ones locked the door, leave with them in the distanct.